Myrtle R Douglas:
Mother of Convention Costuming

About the International Costumers' Guild Press

The International Costumers' Guild Press is the publication arm of the non-profit International Costumers' Guild (ICG). Its mission is to publish long-form content including books and monographs on topics related to costumes and costuming.

The ICG is an affiliation of hobbyist and professional costumers, dedicated to the promotion and education of costuming, including cosplay, as an art form in all its aspects. The ICG Press serves the ICG's mission as a non-profit educational organization.

For more information about the ICG and to locate a chapter near you, visit its website: *https://www.costume.org*.

If you have an idea for a book or a manuscript that is ready for publication, contact the Editor in Chief at *icgpress-editor@costume.org*.

International
Costumers' Guild
Press

Myrtle R Douglas

Mother of Convention Costuming

The International Costumers' Guild pays homage to the fan who forever influenced what we wear at sci-fi/fantasy conventions.

Philip Gust

Copyright © 2025 by the International Costumers' Guild, Inc.

All rights reserved. No part of this work may be reproduced in any manner without the express written consent of the copyright holder, except in the case of brief quotations embedded in critical articles and reviews.

Requests for permission to reproduce material from this work should be sent to the ICG Press at *icgpress-editor@costume.org*.

No AI Training: Without in any way limiting the exclusive rights of the copyright holder, any use of this publication to "train" generative artificial intelligence (AI) technologies to generate text is expressly prohibited. The copyright holder reserves all rights to license uses of this work for generative AI training and development of machine learning language models.

Produced in the United States of America.
Publication Date: January 2025.
Publisher: International Costumers' Guild Press.
Research: Kathleen Gust.
Cover Design: Philip Gust.

ISBN *978-1-966384-03-8* (Softcover)
ISBN *978-1-966384-04-5* (Hardcover)

Library of Congress Control Number: 2024953069

.

"Playing Dress-up begins at
age five and never truly ends."

Kate Spade

FOREWORD

Today, we take it for granted that fans of sci-fi/fantasy dress as their favorite characters from movies, TV, and literature. But the phenomenon only began with the advent of sci-fi/fantasy conventions late in the first half of the 20th century. In fact, it started with two fans from California who attended the first World Science Fiction Convention, later called Nycon 1, in New York City during the summer of 1939.

One was a young man named Forrest J Ackerman, and the other was his friend, Myrtle R Douglas, also an enthusiastic fan of sci-fi literature. They were members of the Los Angeles Science Fantasy Society (LASFS), the first in the U.S. To the surprise of other attendees, both wore costumes created by Douglas, inspired by futuristic garments in a recent sci-fi film. They attracted a lot of attention as they greeted and interacted with fellow attendees. Other fans embraced the idea, and wearing costumes at sci-fi/fantasy conventions soon grew in popularity.

Ackerman enjoyed a long and illustrious career in sci-fi/fantasy fandom and became a celebrity and media personality. Although she was also well-known among sci-fi/fantasy literature fans at the time, Douglas did not rise to the same level of prominence, and her legacy as the first costumer at a sci-fi/fantasy convention is almost unknown today.

The International Costumers' Guild (ICG) had made a special presentation to Ackerman, in 1994 recognizing him as the "Father of Convention Costuming" at Conadian, the 52nd Worldcon in Winnipeg Canada. It was made to Ackerman in person by then ICG President Pierre Pettinger. Since Ackerman was so well known, little background about him or the reason for the award was needed. However, memory about Douglas had faded, and no mention her contribution was made.

In April 2016, the ICG Pat and Peggy Kennedy Memorial Archives team submitted a proposal to the ICG Board to recognize Douglas as the "Mother of Convention Costuming" for creating and wearing the first costumes at a sci-fi/fantasy convention and her efforts to popularize convention costuming. The ICG board approved the motion in May 2016 and a presentation was scheduled to take place at MidAmeriCon II, the 74th Worldcon in Kansas City, Missouri in August 2016.

As then current ICG President, I would not be able to make a similar presentation to Douglas in person because she passed away in 1964. Instead, I decided to create a documentary video about her contributions to sci-fi/fantasy costuming, and announcing the ICG's recognition. My hope was that the video would continue to inform people, even after the presentation has been made.

This book commemorates Douglas's contributions to convention costuming and tells her story. The video is available on YouTube. (*https://youtube.com/watch?v=DasGQQkj-xY*) An article about making the video appeared in *The Virtual Costumer* magazine, vol. 17, issue 2 in 2019. (*https://siwcostumers.org/vc_contents.html#v17_i2*)

A Special Award Presentation
at the 74th World Science Fiction Convention

Caravan Hall, on the third floor of this building on 59th Street in Manhattan.

THE PRESENTATION

Hello. I'm Philip Gust, President of the International Costumers' Guild.

For over 30 years, the ICG, and its chapters and members, have been dedicated to the promotion and education of costuming as an art form in all its aspects. The ICG Guidelines for Ensuring Fair Competition, have been adopted by convention masquerades worldwide.

Conventions are a favorite place for costumers to show off their skills. In fact, the tradition of convention costuming began in Caravan Hall, on the third floor of this building on 59th Street in Manhattan. It was here in 1939 that Nycon I, the very first World Science Fiction Convention, was held.

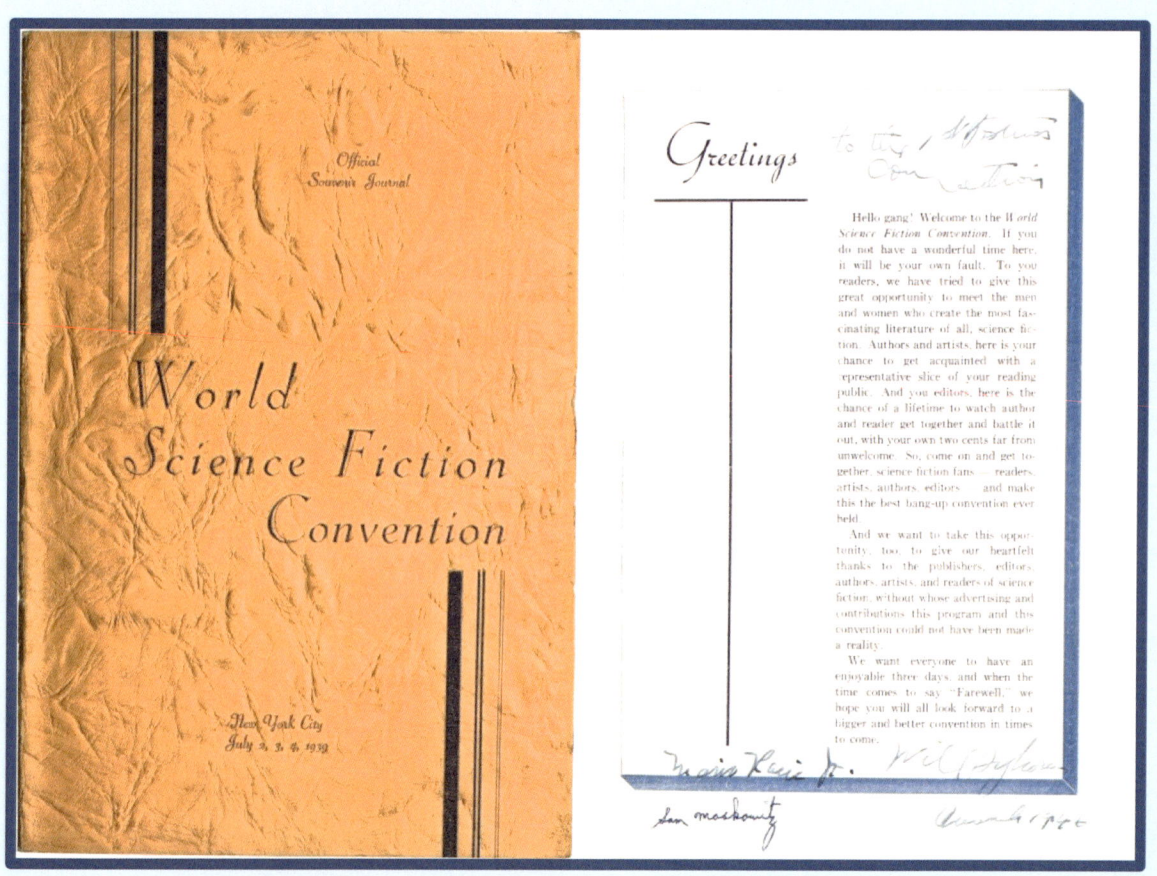

World Science Fiction Convention (Nycon I) program book.

On that sweltering July 2nd opening day, you couldn't help noticing a tall young man stationed at the entrance, greeting attendees in fluent Esperanto.

He was decked out in what he called a "futuristicostume," with a green satin cape, peg pants and a yellow long-sleeve button-down shirt

Forrest J Ackerman wearing "futuristicostume" at Nycon 1 in 1939

It was inspired by costumes from the 1936 science fiction film feature, "Things to Come," adapted from a book by H. G. Wells

On the front of the shirt, in green letters, was his nickname, "4SJ."

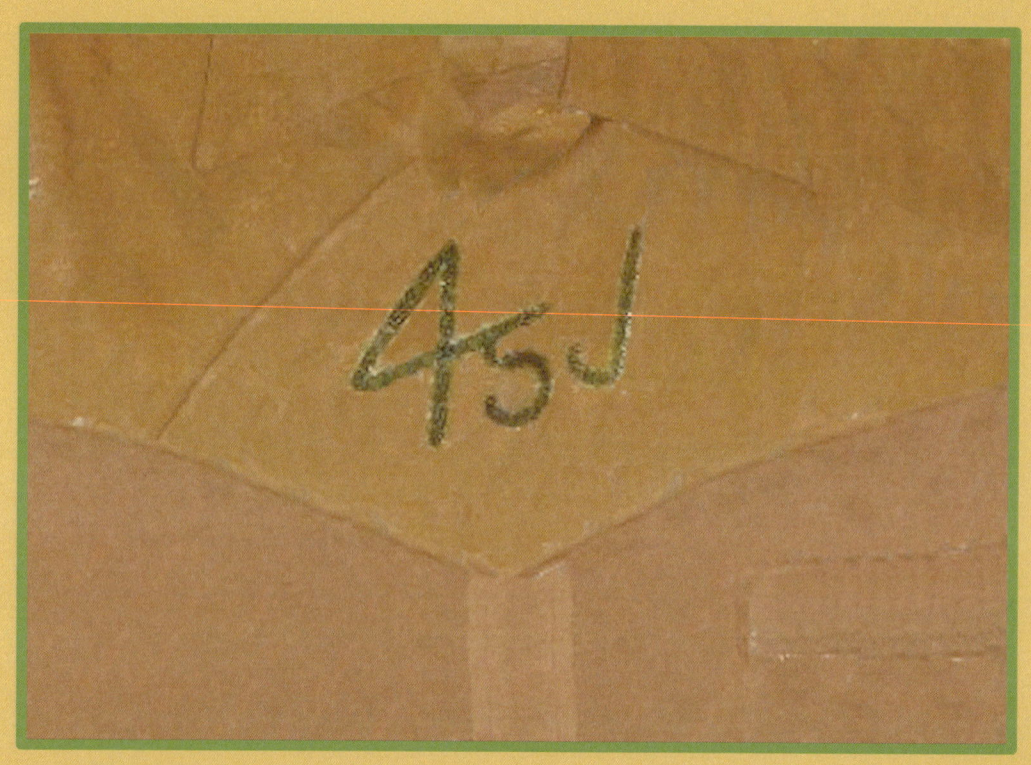

Ackerman's nickname was on his shirt in green letters.

Publicity photo from "Things to Come" (1936).

But Forrest J Ackerman wasn't the only costumed attendee. Standing next to him on that hot New York day, and also greeting attendees in Esperanto, was Myrtle R Douglas, better known in science fiction circles by her Esperanto name, Morojo (Mo-ro'yo).

It was Morojo who had envisioned, designed, and laboriously hand-made Ackerman's "futuristi-costume" for that first Worldcon, as well as her own space-age gown that cleverly converted into a cape-romper combo

Forrest J Ackerman and Myrtle R Douglas wear their "futuristicostumes" at Nycon1 in 1939.

Los Angeles Science Fantasy Society members.

She and Ackerman shared a passion for Esperanto, and science fiction, and they were both members of the Los Angeles Science Fantasy Society, the oldest sci-fi fan club.

They started its fan zine, "Voice of the Imagi-Nation" and co-edited 50 issues between 1938 to 1947.

Morojo remained active for many years, publishing zines, and creating costumes that she wore to conventions.

Publishing "Voice of Imagi-Nation" fan-zine.

Douglas remained active for many years.

According to Ackerman,

"In 1940 at the first Chicon she & I put on a skit based on some dialog from "Things to Come," and won some kind of a prize.

"In 1941 at the Denvention she wore a Merrittesque AKKA-mask (frog face) devised by the then young & as yet unknown master filmonster model maker & animator, Ray Harryhausen.

"In 1946 at the Pacificon in LA, I understand she created a sensation as A. Merritt's 'Snake Mother.'"

Ackerman and Douglas put on a skit and won some kind of prize at the first Chicon in 1940

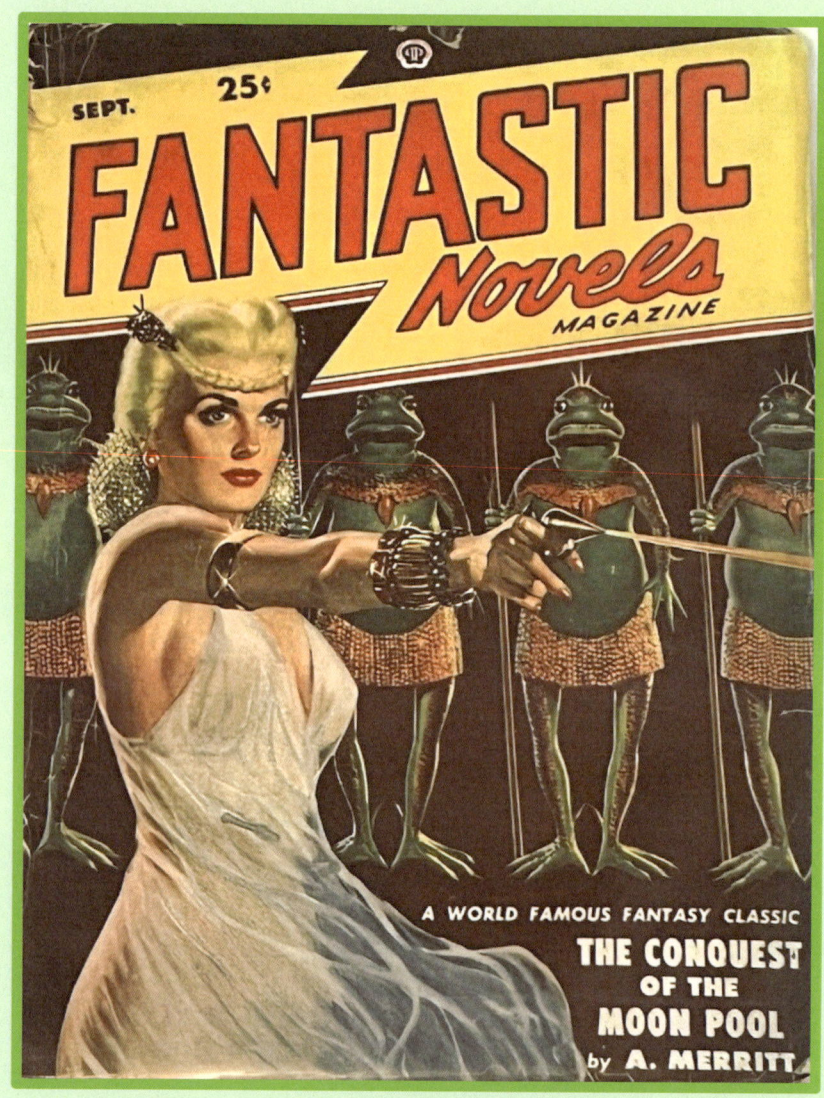

Douglas wore a frog-face AKKA-mask designed by Ray Harryhausen at 1941 Denvention.

Douglas created a sensation at 1946 Pacificon in LA as A. Merritt's "Snake Mother."

The ICG recognized Forrest J Ackerman as the "Father of Convention Costuming" at ConAdian in 1994.

At ConAdian, the 52nd Worldcon in Winnipeg Canada in 1994, ICG President Pierre Pettinger presented a plaque to Forrest J Ackerman, recognizing him as the "Father of Convention Costuming" for wearing his "futuristicostume" at the first Worldcon.

I'm pleased to announce at MidAmeriCon II, the 74th Worldcon in Kansas City, Missouri in 2016, that the ICG recognizes Myrtle R Douglas as the "Mother of Convention Costuming" for creating both "futuristicostumes" and wearing one of them at the first Worldcon.

Thank you, Morojo, for your energy and enthusiasm for the art form, and for helping to establish convention costuming as the worldwide phenomenon we know today.

The ICG recognized Myrtle R Douglas as the "Mother of Convention Costuming" at MidAmericaCon II in 2016.

AFTERWORD

After the video played at the MidAmeriCon II masquerade halftime, I was so happy with the audience's reception. One person later posted a message that they thought it was a warm and loving tribute to Douglas. Another said they liked that her work had been recognized and to hear just how old this form of costuming actually is. It was especially satisfying knowing that the video brought Douglas' contributions to light, and finally gave her the recognition that she deserved.

I am grateful to the ICG Archives team for proposing that the ICG recognize Myrtle R Douglas for her contributions to costuming, and for providing me the opportunity to get to know her and to create a documentary video and a book that tells her story to the costuming community.

Thanks also to MidAmeriCon II for allowing the ICG to present this award and show the video at the convention.

Finally, I especially want to thank my wife Kathleen Gust for her time and expertise in researching Douglas, finding obscure sources, and locating many of the images. The video and this book would not have been possible without her.

ACKNOWLEDGEMENTS

I would like to acknowledge and thank the following people, organizations, and sources for their help and the material used in the original video presentation and in this commemorative book.

Research: Katheen Gust

Ackerman/Douglas images: ICG Pat and Peggy Kennedy Memorial Archives

Caravan Hall image: New York Public Library

LASFS images: Los Angeles Science Fantasy Society

Ackerman appreciation document: Efanzines.com ("I Remember Morojo")

Futuristicostume shirt image: Yourprops.com

Nycon I Program image: Animecons.com

ABOUT MYRTLE REBECCA ("MOROJO") DOUGLAS

Myrtle Rebecca Douglas was born on June 20, 1904 in Phoenix, Arizona to Robert Douglas and Lillie Dell (Kilpatrick) Schutz.

Douglas became heavily involved with the Los Angeles sci-fi/fantasy community and was active in the Los Angeles Science Fantasy Society in the 1930s and 1940s. She was also involved with the Esperanto movement, as were many in the sci-fi/fantasy community at the time, including Forrest J Ackerman.

Douglas was a little older than many members, and often provided an ear to younger members who sought her guidance. She served in various roles, including as newsletter editor, treasurer, and president.

In 1939, Douglas and several other members, including Ackerman and a young Ray Bradbury, decided to travel by train from Los Angeles to Nycon I, the first sci-fi/fantasy convention. Ackerman later stated that they thought everyone was supposed to wear a costume at a science fiction convention, and were surprised that they were the only ones who did. Douglas continued to make and wear costumes at sci-fi/fantasy conventions throughout the 1940s.

Douglas died in the early morning of November 30, 1964 in Patton, San Bernadino County, California after a long illness. She was survived by her niece Patti Gray ("Pogo"), and her son Virgil Roger Smith Douglas. Her passing was mourned by her friends in the Los Angeles sci-fi/fantasy community, who fondly remembered the pleasure of her company and the inspiration of her life.

ABOUT THE AUTHOR

Philip Gust enjoys sci-fi and fantasy costuming, and has particular interests in props, special effects, and prosthetic makeup. He also costumes in historical periods, including Regency, Victorian, and early 20th C. He has co-directed costume masquerades at the local and regional level, and served as a judge at the local, regional, and international levels.

He served as ICG President from 2012 to 2017. He currently chairs the ICG Publications Committee and the ICG Technology Committee, and serves as the ICG Webmaster. He is the founding Editor in Chief of the ICG Press (*https://costume.org/wp/icg-press/*).

As a member of the Silicon Web Costumers' Guild chapter, he is the Editor of the chapter's *The Virtual Costumer* quarterly online magazine (*https://siwcostumers.org/vc*), and hosts the "Silicon Web Costumers' Guild Presents" webinar series (*https://siwcostumers.org/webinars*).

He and wife Kathleen Gust received the ICG Lifetime Achievement Award in 2021. The award is the ICG's highest honor, recognizing a body of achievement in the costuming art and service to the costuming community. (*https://costume.org/wp/icg-lifetime-achievement-award/*).

He holds a Master of Science degree in Computer Science, and a Bachelor of Science degree in Mathematics and Psychology. He has worked on NASA space missions that have visited every planet in the solar system.

www.ingramcontent.com/pod-product-compliance
Ingram Content Group UK Ltd.
Pitfield, Milton Keynes, MK11 3LW, UK
UKRC030653250125
454025UK00005B/13